Photomontage

Photomontage

Experimental Photography Between the Wars

Introduction
by Michel Frizot

Thames and Hudson

Note

This book is deliberately restricted to coverage
of works made between 1918 and 1939.
It includes works made up of photographic prints
cut up, reassembled, sometimes complemented
by painted additions, and works made up of
several superimposed negatives.
It should be noted that certain of
these images use colour.

Translated from the French by Shaun Whiteside

On the cover: László Moholy-Nagy, *Death on the Rails*, c. 1925,
New York, Museum of Modern Art

First published in Great Britain in 1991 by
Thames and Hudson Ltd, London
Originally published in France by the Centre National de la Photographie
Copyright © 1987 by Centre National de la Photographie, Paris
English translation copyright © 1991 by Thames and Hudson Ltd, London

Printed and bound in Italy

THE LYING CAMERA

'Looking on my enterprise as a sort of photomontage and choosing for my expression a tone as objective as possible, trying to gather my life into a single solid block ... I was imposing on myself a rule quite as severe as if I had intended to compose a classical work.... To use materials of which I was not the master and which I had to take as I found them..., such was the risk I accepted and the law I had fixed for myself.' Prompted by the 'desire to *expose myself* (in every sense of the term)', it was with reference to photomontage that French anthropologist and author Michel Leiris justified the jumble of memories liable to disconcert the reader of his ethnological autobiography, *L'Âge d'homme*.[1] His words date from 1939, twenty years into the flourishing of an experimental technique that was often discredited or denigrated as one of the applied arts. In attempting, first of all, to describe the illogical method he employed to decode memories and childhood, Leiris was also, indirectly, providing a brief definition of photomontage: a work produced by rules both severe and classical, assembling prefabricated material in a tangible and objective 'block'. While the writer chose psychoanalytic introspection as a means of escaping from hell, the *photomonteur* of the twenties also dived into the chaotic unconscious of collective images to bring back the pearls of a rediscovered illusionism originally produced, in the early years of the century, by the phantasmagorias of magic-lantern shows and the cinematic tricks of Méliès.

Other machines for dreaming, for reconstructing the world, were still to be invented – machines yet more tactile, organic and implacable. Their workings, if not their tricks, were yet to be exposed, just as Michel Leiris exposed his anodine intimacies to the public eye. Photomontage is one of those illusionistic mechanisms, fuelled by a new and invisible energy, which set in motion the hitherto immobile space of the white page like those robotic psychoportraits that Picabia was drawing around 1916.

With photomontage, photography, which had so far been considered dignified only in the field of pictorialism, became integrated within the century's avant-garde movements thanks to a deviation, geared towards revolutionary ends, of the principles of spatial structuring created by Cubism. Born in 1916, the progeny of Grosz and Heartfield, and again in Berlin in 1918 in the Dada group formed around Raoul Hausmann, Hannah Höch and Johannes Baader, photomontage was the heir to Braque's *trompe-l'oeil* collages (1910), and the *papiers collés* and typographical fragments used by Picasso (1911-12). It represented an escape into abstraction (Picasso, Sonia Delaunay, Arp) and a return to the figuration (however fragmentary) of reality in the form of wallpaper, newspapers, cigarette packets, resembling courtroom exhibits, glued straight on to the surface. The Futurists had already subverted these fine principles with their '*parole libere*' and Balla's *Interventionist Manifesto* (1914), made up of passages cut from other texts. 'The assemblage and combination of expressive elements drawn from photographs' (Stepanova, 1928) photomontage emerged into the furiously recriminative environment of Dada as 'a new unity which extricated, from the chaos of war and revolution, a visually and conceptually new visionary reflection',[2] 'such that one might say in pictures what would have been immediately censored in words' (Grosz). Between 1920 and 1922, Dadaist agitation was the chief source for these images; Max Ernst, in Cologne, to some extent blunted the edge of Dadaism with his 'photo-paintings' (1921), softening its denunciatory tendencies in favour of formal, narrative, poetic qualities. He tempered the Dadaist tone with the vague, floating space of the painted background, with forms floating independently and incongruously against it.

From 1922, photomontage was propelled into the field of graphic and expressive novelties by centres of production such as Moscow and the Weimar Bauhaus (and in Dessau from 1925 onwards). One of the propaganda works of the new media, *Malerei, Fotografie, Film*, published by Moholy-Nagy at the Bauhaus in 1925 as a vindication of the applied arts, typography, the photogram (it was at this point that the 'new photography' entered the scene), reproduced photomontages by Höch, Citroen (*Metropolis*), an American advertisement and four 'photosculptures' by Moholy. It was subsequently in the applied arts (posters, advertising, page layout), that photomontage found its calling within the mass media: posters by Tschichold, propaganda by Rodchenko, political satires by Heartfield.

Originally, the word *Fotomontage* itself 'conveyed our hatred for artists. . . . Seeing ourselves more as engineers, we wanted to build, to assemble [*montieren*] our works' (R. Hausmann).[3] If the new form was geared towards destructive ends within the politico-artistic sphere, it was also seen as constructive, an act of manufacture, a transformation of basic materials. The word "photomontage" is the product of industrial culture – the assembly of machines and turbines'.[4] The *photomonteur* is an image-mechanic, assembling separate parts to produce a message, a directly communicable work.

There is no real definition of photomontage. It is basically a practice which includes photography as one of the materials of a composite image, complemented by planes, lines, cut-outs, *objets trouvés*, and also incorporating the printing of two superimposed negatives. The photomontage can then be photographed and printed, thus producing a flat surface that eliminates the unevenness of the cut-out or collage. Many photomontages became known only through their reproduction in magazines. The photomontage avoids the elitism of the unique work. It claims to be a multiple product, like the photograph.[5] Photomontage has no rules other than that of its own autonomy. It occupies the free space opened up by the visual avant-garde movements such as Futurism, Dada, Constructivism, Suprematism and Productivism, in the overexcited Europe of the twenties when, from Paris to Moscow, ideas travelled at the speed of locomotives, along with men, books, pamphlets and exhibitions. Photomontage adapted to the given landscape of the visual arts, lending it its crude and photographically realistic images, its glimpses of truth, according to the message it sought to convey.

'Photomontage enables us to develop the most highly dialectical formulae because of its conflicts in terms of structure and dimension, between the rough and the smooth, for example, the aerial view and the foreground, perspective and flatness' (R. Hausmann).[6] The move was towards dynamic simplification, from the apocalyptic reconstruction of *Metropolis* to the evocation of that limitless expanse of antiperspective, furnished with fragile and transparent structures, of Malevich's Suprematism, sometimes producing a unique, decentred and low-angled photograph. It was at this point that the *photomonteur* became a photographer. It was no longer enough for him to cut up magazines or press-agency photographs. He wanted to create his own material, perhaps simply inverting the traditional photographic framework, using a portable camera: by overturning and perspectively inverting the subject he obtained the unexpected and destabilizing effect of photomontage. Thus it was, at all events, that Rodchenko became a photographer in 1924, and that was also the reason why Moholy-Nagy suddenly took up photography in 1925, supported by his wife Lucia, and became a master of the 'new vision'.

Moholy himself was well aware, as a result of his fairly brief involvement with photomontage, of this development which led from anarchistic denunciation to the carefully typeset propaganda of the thirties. Starting out in 1922 in a style close to the organized chaos of Schwitters' *Merz*, accumulations of found junk and meaningless fragments, he very soon brought to photomontage the structure of the painted 'constructions' he was making at the time, very sparse geometric compositions with multiple vanishing points close to El Lissitzky's *Proun*. This created fluid white spaces in which a few lines, circles and axes produced the depth of a yawning gap in which a few photographic cutouts, human and animal, floated serenely. Moholy himself made the following comment on *Leda and the Swan* (1925): 'Linear elements, structural pattern, close-up, and isolated figures are here the elements for a space articulation. Pasted on a white surface these elements seem to be embedded in infinite space, with clear articulation of nearness and distance. The best description of their effect would be perhaps to say that each element is pasted on vertical glass panes, which are set up in endless series each behind the other.'[7] The visual theory of the twenties was not concerned with reproducing familiar sights, but with producing new visions. And photomontage certainly allowed for that. From 1924, Moholy applied the technique to photographic posters, and his photomontage *Männerserie*, along with an advertising slogan, became the poster for the Schocken chain of shops (1927). Starting out with leaflets,[8] he made eight covers for the fashion magazine *die neue linie* (1929-33). From its humble origins in collage, photomontage went on, via Moholy's example, to produce that graphic style that has dominated modern page layout since the 1930s.

Three visual 'events' reveal the European fashion for photomontage a decade into its existence: the publication of *foto-auge / oeil et photo / photo-eye* by Roh and Tschichold in 1929, the massive exhibition 'Film und Foto' in Stuttgart, organized the same year by Moholy-Nagy, and finally the exhibition 'Fotomontage', which consecrated the medium, at the Berlin Kunstgewerbemuseum in 1931, organized by César Domela (catalogue with essays by Domela and Klucis). Despite having a self-portrait photomontage by El Lissitzky on the cover, *foto-auge* was chiefly devoted to the German group and the 'object-fantasticality, in which from simple fragments of reality a more complex unit is piled up'.[9] In the exhibition 'Film und Foto', it was evident that photomontage had already become a part of the work of most of the German participants (although it was absent from the photography of the French and the Americans, represented in the exhibition by Kertész, Tabard, Florence Henri, Stieglitz, Steichen, etc.). Two groups of institutions were apparent: the art schools (the Folkwangschule, Essen; the Meisterschule, Munich; and the Kunstgewerbeschule, Stuttgart), and particularly the 'block' of anonymous Russians led by El Lissitzky.[10] Graphic artists from across the whole of Europe (including the Frenchman Maximilien Vox) had entered the lists under the banner of photomontage. The technical terms, however, did little to conceal the diversity of conceptions and applications: the 'phototypographies' of Schuitema, Tschichold, etc., Moholy's 'photoplastiques', let alone the works of Heartfield, described as 'Foto-Grafik', 'Foto-Satire', 'Foto-Plakat', and 'Foto-Einbände'.[11]

In the USSR, photomontage was also one of the warhorses of revolutionary art in the service of ideology, propaganda through pictures. Klucis, Rodchenko, El Lissitzky and the Stenberg brothers were adherents of Productivism,[12], which learned a great deal from the shortcomings of Constructivism, considered too abstract to reach the masses. Obeying the Party's injunctions to make the message easily accessible to the workers, these artists found in applied photography a substitute for the 'imperfect methods of drawing' to convey 'the mechanical complexity of the outward forms of objects and our industrial culture'. In 1923 Rodchenko worked on his series of photomontages for the collection *Pro Eto (Of This)* by Mayakovsky, before taking up the design of pamphlets, posters and book-covers, always using photomontage. For him, photographic fragments were the visual equivalents of words. The photomontages in *Pro Eto*, which are like literal illustrations to the poems, include symbols, 'verisms' (for example, a telephone number), and even the portrait of Mayakovsky.

As regards the return to realism and the object, Klucis was one of those responsible for the success of a form of photomontage which 'was not merely a collection of photographs, [and] had to be accompanied by political slogans, colours and graphic elements'. Starting out in 1920 with photographic collages of little figures of workers on Suprematist paintings, Klucis went on to produce the postcards for the Moscow Spartakiades (1928), and the posters for the first Five-Year Plan (1930). Rodchenko designed a large number of covers for the political magazine *Novy Lef* (1927-28), covers for crime paperbacks (*Miss Mend*, 1924) and other books. El Lissitzky, who was also fighting his campaign on every available front, in 'pure' painting, architecture and design, introduced himself, in his 1924 photomontage self-portrait, as a typographer and 'constructor'. He very quickly came to use photographic enlargements for the design and arrangement of exhibitions (Dresden, 1926; Hanover, 1927; 'Pressa', Cologne, 1928), and also produced book covers (*The USSR Under Construction*, 1933).

Around the two poles of the Bauhaus and the Russian avant-garde there hovered many artists who expressed themselves chiefly by means of these exhibitions. Since graphic art was an almost compulsory phase of Modernism at the time, all young artists (most of whom were also painters) worked on photomontages from 1925 onwards.[13] There were also isolated individuals who could not be diverted from their personal paths, such as John Heartfield who found photomontage an ideal means of expression, reaching a wide audience through magazines such as the *Arbeiter Illustrierte Zeitung*, followed by the *Volks Illustrierte*, for which he designed a large number of covers (some thirty-five between 1930 and 1938). He had previously designed covers for the Malik-Verlag (Berlin 1921-23). Because of his socialist, anti-militarist and Dadaist beliefs, Heartfield was most particularly a fierce and tireless denouncer of Fascism and its underhand allegiances. With the addition of short texts or captions designed to explain, reinforce or stress the satire of the images, his photomontages picture a fictional reality, but one no more improbable for that, exploring 'the lost path of mystery in daily life'[14] to reveal the horror of the invisible lie.

Having originated in Dada and been co-opted by Constructivism, photomontage, which did not adhere to any aesthetic except that of free association, spread to many different European artistic groups and movements. In the twenties and thirties *photomonteurs* were to be found in Poland (Berman, Brzeski, Podsadecki), Hungary (Kessak, Lengyel) and particularly among the Italian Futurists, at the very heart of Modernism, with Pannaggi (close to Hausmann, 1924-27), Boccardi, Demanins, Fillia, Pacetti, Vottero, Paladini (the most Constructivist), Tato (superimposed negatives) and Wanda Wulz,[15] who produced the extraordinary *Me + Cat* (1932). The French branch of this 'Internationale' developed in a more literary way in Breton's Surrealism, rejecting both Dada and Constructivism. The Surrealist photomontages were supposed to be dream images, realizations of Lautréamont's 'chance encounter on a dissecting table of an umbrella and a sewing-machine'. Max Ernst, Léo Malet and Georges Hugnet produced real *'histoires montées'*, while Tabard and Roger Parry used superimposed negatives.[16] But the influence of photomontage was felt primarily among the poster-designers (Carlu and Cassandre both used the technique), and in the design of weekly magazines: *VU*, set up in 1929, *Regards*, *Miroir du monde* and even *Détective*, which used photographic cut-outs, maskings, overspill, typographical unevenness or Heartfield-like illustrations (covers for *VU* by Alexandre Liberman, satires by Marianus in *Mariane*).[17]

The success of photomontage as an art of communication lies both in its narrative, illustrative calling ('between seeing and hearing', said Hausmann) and its truth-content derived from photographic realism. A manufactured image with its components on display, each claiming its own objective reality, photomontage raised the question of artistic and photographic deception. It reorganized the traditional visual sense and destroyed the trust built up by almost a century of plain, straightforward, pure photography. It was 'that precision, that documentary aspect [which] gave photography a power over the viewer that could not be attained by graphic representation'.[18] The only logic that photomontage obeys is that of referential substitution, in which meaning is cast aside by virtue of the lie inherent in the artefact.

Michel Leiris, once again, said the following of his *L'Age d'homme*, disturbing in its illogical simplicity: 'This work in which are confronted childhood memories, accounts of real events, dreams and actually experienced impressions, in a kind of surrealist collage or rather photomontage, since no element is utilized which is not of strict veracity or of documentary value.'[19] The truth of photomontage does not lie only in the authenticity of its photographic components, their autonomous statements, their cacophonous outspokenness. It can also be produced by the unexpected collision of mutually unfamiliar worlds: 'elements of reality are made recondite by the intermediary of art. Art is not made extraordinary by reality, reality becomes extraordinary through art.'[20]

A Little Prince traversing the planet of photomontage would encounter Dadaists, Constructivists, poster-artists, all of whom would draw, or cut out, a sheep for him, preparing it for the terrifying confrontation with any fox or lamplighter. Belief in the truth of the artistic gesture lies in the imaginary realism of the lie represented. Between Hausmann's abrupt statement: 'I am not a photographer', and Man Ray's punning claim to be a *'fautographe'*, there is room for the suspicion that the invention of Dada photo-montage as a means of disconcerting the viewer was designed to encourage a hope for the emergence of Truth from the lie.

Michel Frizot

1. Michel Leiris, introduction to *L'Age d'homme*, Paris, Gallimard, 1939; English edition: *Manhood*, London, Jonathan Cape, 1968, pp. 19-20.

2. Raoul Hausmann, 'Conférence sur le photomontage', Berlin, 1931, published in *Raoul Hausmann, Je ne suis pas un photographe*, Paris, Chêne, 1975.

3. Raoul Hausmann, in *Courrier dada*, Paris, 1958, p. 42.

4. Gustav Klucis, 1931, quoted by C. Lodder, *Russian Constructivism*, New Haven, London, Yale University Press, 1983, note 34, p. 296.

5. The cover of *Der Dada* no. 3, 1920, is signed 'John Heartfield mont.', after the fashion of '*sculpsit*' in classical prints. *Der Monteur Heartfield* (the name he had assumed by that time), the main motif of which, cut out and stuck on to the work, is a mechanism of gearwheels in place of the heart. Cf. also the collages of Max Ernst, made from *fin-de-siècle* magazine cut-outs, and published in books: *La Femme 100 têtes* and *Une semaine de bonté*, 1934; also, in the same tradition, *La Septième Face du dé* by Georges Hugnet, Paris, Jeanne Bucher, 1936.

6. Raoul Hausmann, *Courrier dada*, Paris, 1958, p. 48.

7. *Space-Time and the Photographer*, 1942, reproduced in *Moholy-Nagy*, ed. Richard Kostelanetz, New York, Praeger, 1970, pp. 57-66.

8. Cover of *Holländische Architektur* by J.J.P. Oud, catalogue of the exhibition 'Film und Foto', 1929; cover of *Das Politische Theater* by Erwin Piscator; poster for the lottery, 1932.

9. *foto-auge* reproduced photomontages by Grosz, Heartfield, Burchartz, Schuitema, Tabard (superimposed image), Mesens, Grosz, Moholy, Heartfield, Höch, Vertov; three 'photo-paintings' by Ernst, a 'photo-drawing' by Baumeister and a pamphlet by Zwart.

10. 'Film und Foto' showed photomontages by Ebneth, Erreil, Flachslander, the Folkwangschule of Essen, Fuchs, Grosz, Hausenblas, Herre, Leistikow, Schwitters, Vordemberghe, Vox, Heartfield, Bayer, Höch and Canis: phototypographies by Fuss, the Munich Meisterschule (Tschichold's class), Niessen, Schuitema, Schwitters, the Stuttgart Kunstgewerbeschule, Tschichold, Zwart; 'photosculptures' by Moholy-Nagy; 'Werbefotos' by Schuitema; book covers by Teige; and various unspecified works by the Soviet group.

11. The 1931 exhibition was made up of three groups: the individuals (almost all of them German), the revolutionary artists of Berlin (a.r.b.k.d.) including Eggert and Alice Lex, and the Soviet group of fourteen artists including Klucis, Lissitzky, Rodchenko and Stenberg.

12. Cf. *Rodtchenko*, collection Photo Poche, no. 23; text by Serge Lemoine.

13. Teige, Sutnar, Bayer, Vox, etc. Also worth mentioning is the cover for the catalogue of the 'Abstracts' exhibition in Berlin, 1926, by Oskar Nerlinger, or the jacket for Renger-Patsch's *Hamburg* by Domela in 1930 to show the organic connection between photomontage and all the avant-garde groups of the day, including De Stijl, via Van Doesburg, and Neue Sachlichkeit in the persons of Roh and Gräff.

14. Louis Aragon, *Les Collages*, Paris, Éditions Hermann, 1965.

15. Giovanni Lista, *Futurismo e Fotografia*, Milan, Multhipla, 1979, and *Photographie futuriste italienne*, Paris, Musée d'Art moderne de la Ville, 1981.

16. Photomontages by Valentin, 1928; by Robert Bresson, 1934; Léo Malet, 1935-36; Nush Éluard, 1943-45. A lover of literary collage, Breton included realist photographic 'non-illustrations' in his book *Nadja*, but in quite incongruous ways, acting as collages.

17. In the sphere of posters and advertising, photomontage occupied a considerably important role in the USSR and in the work of German and Dutch designers: Rodchenko's *Kino-Glas* for Vertov, 1924; *Battleship Potemkin* by Lavinsky, 1925; the same subject by Stenberg, 1929; *The Man with the Movie-Camera* by Stenberg, 1929; posters for the Phoebus Palast, by Tschichold, 1927; a poster by Sutnar in Brno, 1929; posters by Schuitema and Burchartz; it was only after the war that photography became generally used in posters: cf. Dawn Ades, *The 20th Century Poster. Design of the Avant-Garde*, Abbeville Press, New York, 1984.

18. Gustav Klucis, 'Le Photomontage comme nouvel aspect de l'art d'agitation', 1931, in Claude Leclanche-Boulé, *Typographies et Photomontages constructivistes en URSS*, Paris, Éditions Papyrus, 1984, pp. 144-45.

19. Michel Leiris, op. cit., p. 16.

20. Werner Spies, 'Paris-Berlin' exhibition catalogue, Centre Georges Pompidou, Paris, 1978, p. 152.

1. Raoul Hausmann, *ABCD, Portrait of the Artist*, 1923

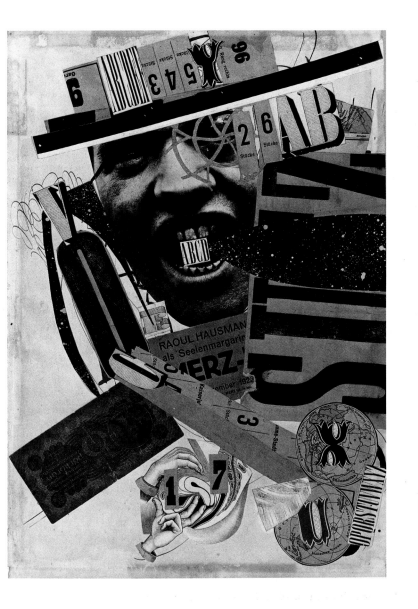

2. Hannah Höch, *Cut with the Carving Knife*, 1919

3. Raoul Hausmann, *Tatlin at Home*, 1920

4. Raoul Hausmann, *The Art Critic*, 1918

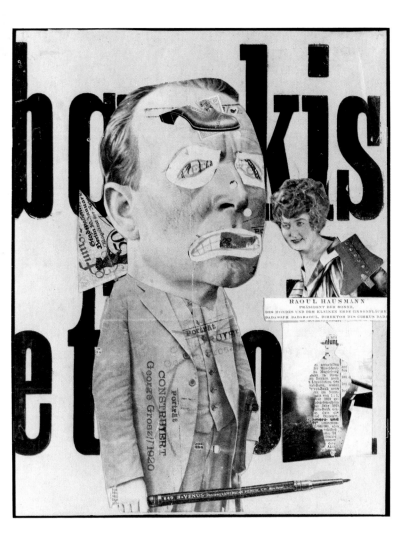

RAOUL HAUSMANN
PRÄSIDENT DER SONNE,
DES MONDES UND DER KLEINEN ERDE (INNENFLÄCHE)
DADASOPH DADARAOUL, DIREKTOR DES CIRKUS DADA

CONSTRUYERT
George Grosz//1920

5. Kurt Schwitters, *Roman Park*, 1934

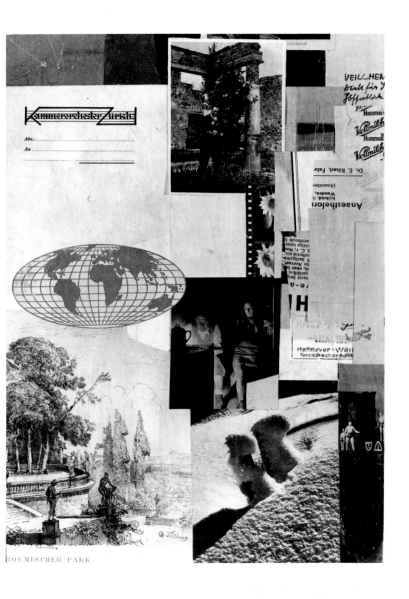

6. Hannah Höch, *César Domela and his Daughter*, 1931

DENKMAL
DES POMELAS UND SEINER TOCHTER

H.H.3

7. Paul Citroen, *Metropolis*, 1923

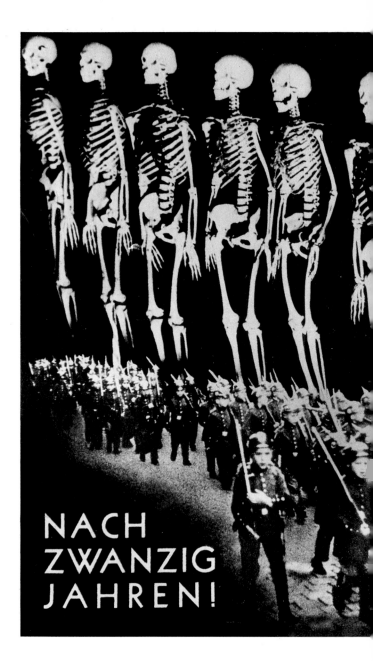

NACH
ZWANZIG
JAHREN!

10. John Heartfield, *The Meaning of Geneva*, *AIZ*, 27 November 1932

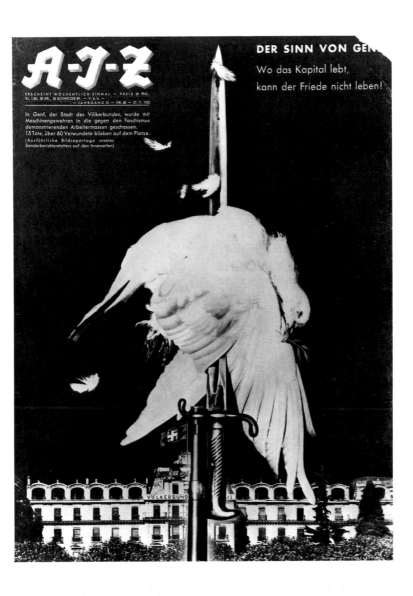

A-I-Z

ERSCHEINT WÖCHENTLICH EINMAL — PREIS 20 PFG.
Kc. 1.60, 20 GR., 30 SCHWEIZER RP. — V. b. b. —
— JAHRGANG XI — NR. 48 — 27. 11. 1932 —

In Genf, der Stadt des Völkerbundes, wurde mit
Maschinengewehren in die gegen den Faschismus
demonstrierenden Arbeitermassen geschossen.
15 Tote, über 60 Verwundete blieben auf dem Platze.
(Ausführliche Bildreportage unseres
Sonderberichterstatters auf den Innenseiten)

DER SINN VON GEN[F]

Wo das Kapital lebt,

kann der Friede nicht leben!

VÖLKERBUND

11. John Heartfield, *Adolf the Superman*, *AIZ*, 17 July 1932

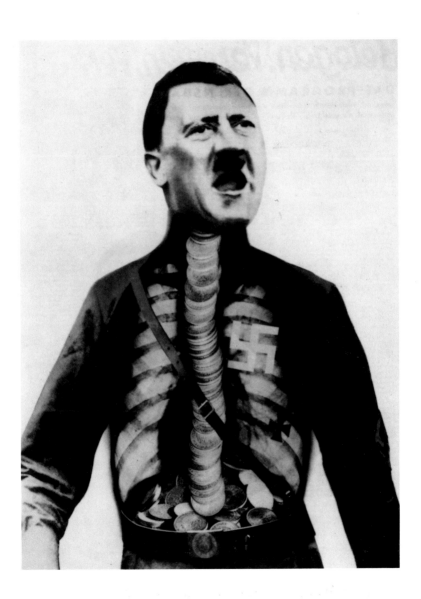

12. John Heartfield, *Madrid*, *AIZ*, 1936

13. John Heartfield, *Brotherhood of Murderers*, undated

AIZ GLEICHE BRÜDER GLEICHE MÖRDER

Berlin, 19. Oktober.
Die italienische faschistische Partei hat dem Stellvertreter
Hitlers, Rudolf Heß, einen Ehrendolch überreichen lassen.

Das Schwarzhemd zum Braunhemd:

„Dir gebührt der Dolch! – Du hast uns im Meuchelmord übertroffen."

Fotomontage: John Heartfield

14. John Heartfield, *The Victory of the Machine*, 1923

FRANZ JUNG

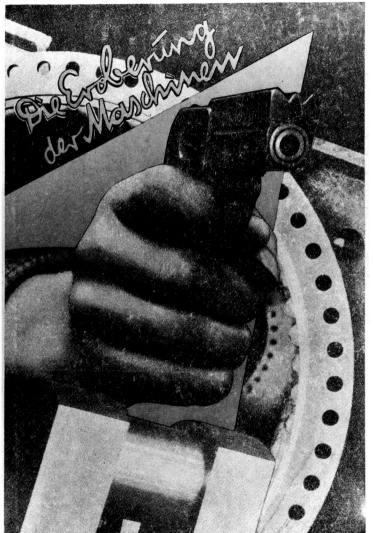

Die Eroberung
der Maschinen

DER MALIK-VERLAG · BERLIN

15. Heinz Hajek-Halke, *Popular Refrain*, 1927

16. Heinz Loew, untitled, 1927-28

17. Alice Lex-Nerlinger, *Dressmaker*, 1930

18. André Steiner, untitled, 1934

19. Heinz Hajek-Halke, *Scandal*, 1932

20. Dziga Vertov, film photomontage, undated

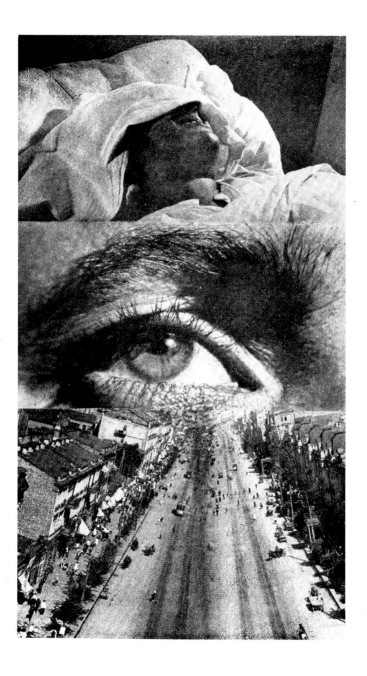

21. Willi Baumeister, photo-drawing, undated

22-23. (Overleaf) Moï Wer, *Ghetto at Osten-Wilna*, undated

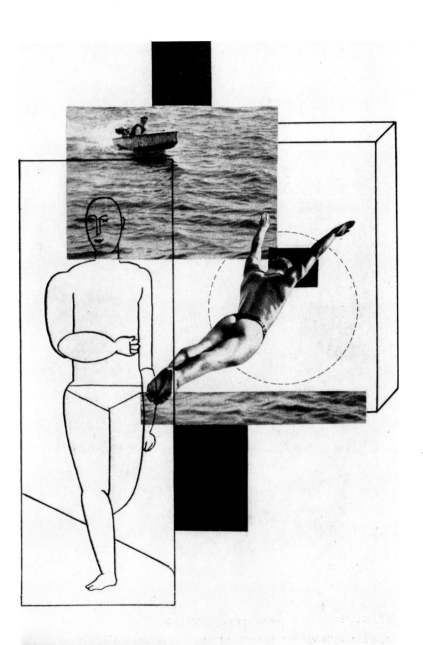

24. (Previous page) Anton Stankowski, *Gas Factory*, 1931
25. César Domela, *Ruths-Speichen*, 1928

26. Piet Zwart, pamphlet, undated

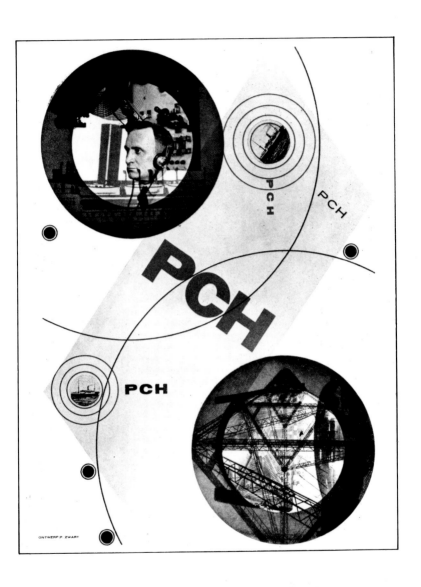

ONTWERP P. ZWART

27. Piet Zwart, catalogue for the 'Dutch Cable Factory', 1928

de papierkabel
op de trekschijf

4 aders worden tot
een kabel geslagen.

1 2 3 4

28. Alexander Rodchenko, cover of the magazine *Novy-Lef*, 1927

N 3

НОВЫЙ
леф

29. El Lissitzky, poster for the Russian exhibition in Zurich, 1929

30-31 (Overleaf) Alexander Rodchenko, extract from *Pro Eto*, poem by Mayakovsky, 1923

Я уши лаплю —
      напрасные мнешь!
слышу
     мой
          мой собственный голос
мне лапы дырявит голоса нож.

В постели она, она лежит, —
Он.
На столе телефон.

32. Gustav Klucis, postcard for the Spartakiades,
Moscow, 1928

33. Gustav Klucis, *Plakatentwurf*, 1931

34-35. (Overleaf) Lajos Lengyel, *Colonialist Politics*, 1933-36, and *Profit*, 1933-36

36. Lajos Lengyel, *This is America*, 1933-36

37. Janusz Maria Brzeski, *20th-century Idyll*, no. 1,
from the cycle 'The Birth of the Robot', 1933

38. Kazimierz Podsadecki, *Women and Children*, 1933

39. Janusz Maria Brzeski, *20th-century Idyll*, no. 4,
from the cycle 'The Birth of the Robot', 1933

40. Janusz Maria Brzeski, *Even Faster*, from the cycle
'The Birth of the Robot', 1933

41. Lajos Kassák, political photomontage, 1930s

42. Lászlò Moholy-Nagy, *Chute*, 1923

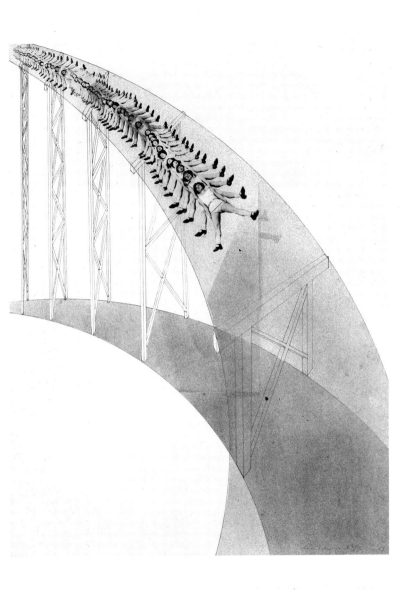

43. László Moholy-Nagy, *The Eternal Feminine*, undated

44. László Moholy-Nagy, *Leda and the Swan*, 1925

45. László Moholy-Nagy, *City Lights*, 1926

Die Lichter der Welt (1925)   Hannah Höch

46. László Moholy-Nagy, *Schoolgirls' Dream*, 1924

47. Lászlò Moholy-Nagy, *Mass Psychosis*, 1927

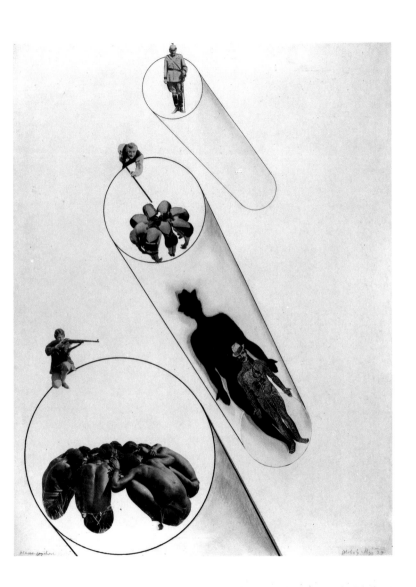

48. Wanda Wulz, *Me + Cat*, 1932

49. Vinicio Paladini, *Movement and Space*, 1928

V. PALADINI

50. Ferruccio A. Demanins, *Marinetti on the Radio*, 1932

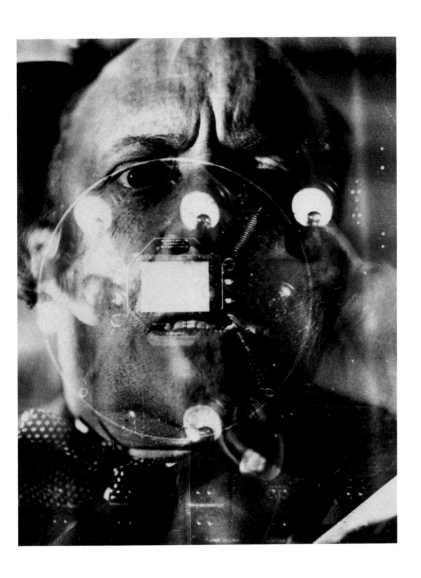

51. End of a Civilization, cover of the magazine *VU*, no. 259, 1 March 1933
52. (Overleaf) Double page of the magazine *VU*, no. 259, 1 March 1933

VU

FIN
D'UNE CIVILISATION

1er MARS 1933
PRIX SPÉCIAL : 6 FRANCS
6e ANNÉE. — N° 255
PARAIT LE MERCREDI
Directeur : LUCIEN VOGEL
Rédacteur en chef : CARLORIM

Photo-montage de M. Ishac

La

Peine des Hommes
Diminue

Grues pivotantes, plus hautes que la Colonne Vendôme, s'avançant de leurs pieds pesants à chenille, portiques aériens qui lèvent à toute allure (jusqu'à 18 m. à la minute) les charges les plus lourdes (400.000 kgs) sont maniés par deux ou trois mécaniciens remplaçant 2.000 êtres humains qui, hier, peinaient sous l'effort, et chôment aujourd'hui faute d'une organisation rationnelle du travail.

53. Roger Parry, untitled, from *Banalités*, 1929

54. Max Ernst, *Loplop Introduces the Members of the Surrealist Group*, 1931

55. Max Ernst, *The Pleiades*, 1921

La puberté proche n'a pas encore enlevé la grâce tenue de nos pléiades / Le regard de nos yeux pleins d'ombre est dirigé vers le pavé qui va tomber / La gravitation des ondulations n'existe pas encore

56. Maurice Tabard, untitled, 1928

57. Maurice Tabard, untitled, 1929

58. Herbert Bayer, *Self-Portrait*, 1932

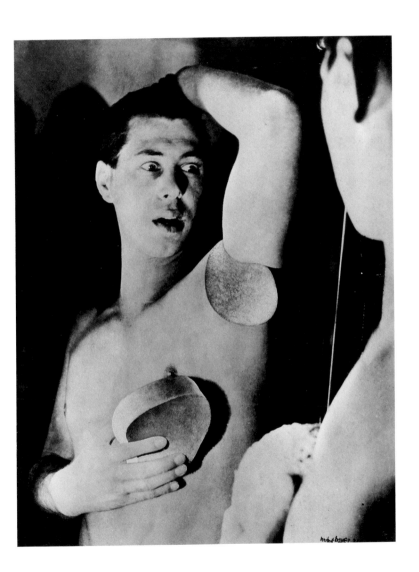

59. Man Ray, *Objects*, 1930

60. Salvador Dali, *The Phenomenon of Ecstasy*,
reproduced in *Minotaure*, no. 3/4, December 1933

THE ANCESTRY OF PHOTOMONTAGE

The technical nature of photography quickly allowed it to be subjected to artificial manipulation. While it was difficult to doctor the daguerreotype – a process which created a single and unique image – the introduction of the negative as an intermediate stage between the taking of the picture and the act of printing made the transformation of the image a possibility. (The calotype process used paper negatives until around 1855, and the subsequent processes involved glass negatives with collodion or albumen, and silver bromide after 1880.) Photomontage, a composite picture made up of autonomous photographic fragments, sometimes complemented by other pictorial means (drawing, painting), became possible once the final image did not

appear directly in the black box but required additional work. The printing of calotype negatives, in which an ill-defined sky could be masked with black gouache or adorned with fake clouds, was already a form of montage, like any excessive retouching which seeks to add elements which do not exist in reality. It was pressure from the elitist medium of painting that brought photography out of its restrictive specificity, the obligation to reproduce what lay before the lens. The tinting of portraits is a product of this imitation of miniatures and paintings.

David Octavius Hill's project, formulated in 1843, to represent on a single canvas 3.45 metres (11 ft 4 in.) long all of the 447 participants in the Congress of the Separation of the Church of Scot-

Anonymous, postcard using a drawn vignette and stuck-on photographs, 1907

land (*The Signing of the Deed of Demission*) reveals the origins of nineteenth-century photomontage. In order to accomplish this ambitious piece of work, Hill turned to photography, and with the aid of Robert Adamson, using the calotype method, he made portraits of those people staying in Edinburgh at the time who were to feature in the finished paint-

Adolphus Pepper, portrait card, c. 1860

ing. The portrait itself was not completed until 1866, but was sufficiently famous to act in the meantime as a model for other works. It brings together, in a sort of amphitheatre, 447 portraits crammed together at random so as not to waste any space, with a fairly artificial perspectival effect obtained by the heads receding in size into the background. This is, technically speaking, a painting copied from photographs. But the earliest known true photomontage derives from the same technique: this is the group portrait of around one hundred citizens of Aberdeen made by G.W. Wilson in 1857 in an arrangement which makes no attempt to

appear natural, and creates a sense of space by means of the variations in scale of the faces without negating their deliberately accumulative effect. This first example is probably derived from the Dutch paintings of corporations and the fashionable caricatures based on the same principle of bringing together a set of faces at random, like the series of 'grimaces' by L.L. Boilly, one of which is photographically reproduced by Fox Talbot in his *Pencil of Nature*, 1844, thus becoming a model for later works.

The same principle was repeated, as part of the fashion for visiting cards and portrait-cards, at the end of the 1850s, by its inventor Disderi, in the form of the 'mosaic card', which he patented on 21 April 1863 when his finances were in decline. The method consisted of cutting out busts of his subjects and glueing them together side by side, then photographing the resulting montage again and printing it in a visiting-card format. In this way it was possible to make 'series of portraits infinite in number . . . and supply businesses with portraits of two or three sitters or up to a thousand, for the same price that we now pay for a card showing a single sitter' (Disderi). It was both an advertisement in catalogue-form for Disderi's work and a game, the purpose of which was to spot and identify the individuals shown. They were brought together with no concern for perspective, simply to create a patchwork effect filling every available space. Using this method, Disderi made a group portrait of 321 celebrities of the Second Empire, arranged in tiers from the peak of a pyramid formed by the Emperor, the Empress and the Imperial Prince; or *The Legs of the Opéra*, a 'Surrealist' collage of medallions portraying the calves of sixty dancers.

This process became fairly commonplace in the 1870s and through to the end of the century for larger-format group portraits; schools, associations, societies and political meetings, both in Europe and the United States. The record was held by Japanese photomontage (of about 1885) which included a total of 1,700 babies' heads.

This playful spirit recurs in the fashion for 'tricks' such as 'spirit' photographs (superimposition of a real portrait and another image already present on the pre-treated negative) in Thiébault's visiting-cards; and in the double self-portraits (sitter playing chess or holding a conversation with himself) through masking; or again, in the pre-Surrealist portraits showing faces on bunches of grapes or in the heart of a flower. Amateur photography, at the end of the century, used all these amusing trick processes, popularizing 'photographic recreations': a big head on a small body, comic scenes constructed with cut-outs, multiple portraits using mirrors.[1] The need for 'veridical' images was such in the 1870s that photographers, secure in their reputation for realism, circulated reconstructions of events which could not be photographed in real life, but which were produced by photomontage. This was the case in the work of Eugène Appert, a specialist in the edifying dramatization of the punishment of the Paris Communards in 1871, which heralded modern photographic disinformation as used in certain countries today.[2]

Anonymous, photomontage portrait, c. 1865

Another tradition of photomontage refers more explicitly to the imitation of painting, or, at least, to products that are visually interesting rather than merely diverting. This trend was launched in London in 1857 with the large photographic 'painting' (78 centimetres [c. 30 in.] long) by Oscar Gustave Rejlander, *The Two Ways of Life*. Modelled on Raphael's *School of Athens*, and featuring an allegory of the paths of honesty and dissipation, Rejlander's composition made use of almost thirty figures or groups photographed separately; it was printed on two joined sheets of paper from some thirty negatives merged together through a masking process. The fame of this piece of technical audacity (bought by Queen Victoria) was primarily due to the avowed rivalry between photography and painting. In this instance, photography triumphed, proving itself capable of producing an image with the same ease and invention as painting; it is also due to the scandal surrounding the proliferation of 'real nudes' which certain contemporaries found far too realistic for comfort. Photography was denounced for its excessive evocative power, which was precisely what modern photomontage was to use to its advantage. During the same period (1856-57), Gustave Le Gray exhibited his sunset or moonlight seaside scenes, using two negatives, one for the sky and the other for the sea, since the sensitivity of collodium to different light intensities made it impossible to capture such a lighting effect on a single plate. Continuing with *Head of John the Baptist* and *Home, Sweet Home*, Rejlander's composite photography was applied more systematically by his disciple H.P. Robinson, with *Fading Away* (1858), *Lady of Shalott* (1861), *Bringing Home the May* (1862), etc., which were highly successful until the arrival of the snapshot. The stated aim was certainly to achieve a painterly effect, which was impossible to attain with a single plate. Robinson's works were preceded by drawn studies on to which he glued photographic fragments. He was concerned with creating a 'self-contained work', not with demonstrating a method that may be of use to painters. This practice led to *fin-de-siècle* pictorialism.[3]

Scrapbooks, such as the Blount album or the Rochester Sackville-West album showing sitters (photographed and cut out) placed more or less naturally in watercolour landscapes, lie somewhere between the search for an artistic effect and personal recreation. Rarer than these, but certainly not unique, is an 'obsession album' of about 1860, comprising photographic collages, recently discovered in Lyons.[4]

Derived from this practice caught between art and play were the photographic postcards, popular at the beginning of the century, that were made by printing a portrait negative superimposed on a drawn vignette. There were various types: *comica* vignettes 'showing characters with grotesque bodies to which the head of a portrait photograph can easily be added', *artista* vignettes, proffering a medallion portrait set in a romantic landscape, *gravura* vignettes (with settings taken from eighteenth-century engravings), *pictura* vignettes and *militaire* vignettes.[5] Military portraits show the soldier in a gleaming uniform, on horseback, in a battlefield, or standing against a background of cannon, surrounded by various patriotic symbols, all in chromolithograph, while only the face is a photograph. According to Hannah Höch's memoirs, it was just such a 'cromo-photo' that gave Raoul Hausmann, in 1917 or 1918, the idea of Dadaist photomontage.

The Dadaist, Surrealist or Constructivist *photomonteur* was thus merely reviving an artistic and recreational practice of the nineteenth century,[6] which already used the tricks quoted by Moholy-Nagy in *Vision in Motion* (1947): superimposed negatives, joining of prints through masking and superimposition of different shots on a single negative. The principle of photomontage was always that of creating a 'dreamed' image, impossible to stage in reality, and thus to subvert real vision with a white lie.

M.F.

1. Gaston Tissandier, *Les Merveilles de la photographie*, Paris, Hachette, 1874.
A. Bergeret and F. Drouin, *Les Récréations photographiques*, Paris, Charles Mendel, 1893.
Charles Chaplot, *La Photographie récréative et fantaisiste*, Paris, Charles Mendel, 1904.

2. Alain Jaubert, *Le Commissariat aux archives*, Paris, Barrault, 1986.

3. H.P. Robinson, *Pictorial Effect in Photography*, 1869.

4. *An Obsession Album*, New York, Daniel Wolf Gallery, September-October 1985.

5. Photo Hall catalogue, Paris, 1917.

6. Robert Sobieszek, 'A Note on Early Photomontage Images', *Image*, XV/4, December 1972, pp. 22-4; R. Sobieszek, 'Composite Imagery and the Origins of Photomontage', *Art Forum*, September 1978, pp. 58-65 and October 1978, pp. 40-45.

Disderi, *The Legs of the Opéra*,
photo-mosaic, 1864

BIOGRAPHIES

Bold figures in brackets refer to plate nos.

Willi Baumeister (1899-1955). German. Typographer, designer, he became a teacher of graphic design at Frankfurt School of Art in 1928. A Constructivist painter, he was a member of Circle and Square (1930) and Abstraction-Creation (1932). Declared a 'degenerate artist' by the Nazis, he lost his teaching post (**21**).

Herbert Bayer (1900-85). Austrian. Student at the Bauhaus from 1921 until 1923, he taught graphic design and advertising graphics from 1925 until 1928. Also an architect, he was very interested in photography during the 1930s. A graphic designer in Berlin until 1938, he finally emigrated to the USA (**58**).

Janusz Maria Brzeski (1907-57). Polish. A typographer, he stayed in Paris in 1925, then in 1929 and 1930. He worked on *VU*, and made his first collages. Returning to Poland, he organized an international photographic exhibition with Podsadecki. He designed numerous page make-ups after 1945 (**37, 39, 40**).

Paul Citroen (1896-1983). Dutch, born in Germany. He made his first photomontages in 1919. He associated with the German Dadaists, and then studied painting at the Weimar Bauhaus, before opening a photographic studio in Berlin, with Umbo. He then taught in Amsterdam and later in The Hague (**7**).

Salvador Dalí (1904-89). Spanish. After studying art in Madrid, and reading Freud, which led him towards 'metaphysical painting', he moved to Paris where he met Picasso, Breton, Miró and Buñuel and joined the Surrealist group; in the 1930s he developed his method of 'critical paranoia', became interested in photography and made photomontages. Expelled from the Surrealists in 1934, he moved to the USA between 1940 and 1948 before returning to Spain (**60**).

Berrucio Demanins (1903-44). Italian, self-taught, he devoted himself to photography in the mid-1920s, opening a studio in Trieste, the city of his birth. He joined the Futurists in 1932; he then made a large number of photomontages by superimposing negatives. He was killed during the bombing of Trieste in 1944 (**50**).

César Domela (b. 1900). Dutch. A self-taught painter who made his first abstract works in 1922. In Paris, in 1924, he joined the De Stijl movement with Mondrian and Van Doesburg, but soon distinguished himself with relief paintings and the use of new materials. He made a series of photomontages in 1929 (**25**).

Max Ernst (1891-1976). A French painter of German origin, he was an active member of the Cologne Dadaists along with Hans Arp, before arriving in Paris in 1920. Very close to the Surrealists, he began a fruitful period of collages, frottages, prints, photomontages and collage novels (including the famous *Femme 100 têtes*, 1929), various techniques that he also applied in his paintings. In 1941 he emigrated to the USA, where he influenced young American painters, and only returned to France in 1955 (**54, 55**).

Heinz Hajek-Halke (1898-1983). German, born in Berlin. A teacher at the Kunstgewerbeschule in Charlottenburg in

1925, he taught photography, made his first photomontages and also worked for Press-Photo in Berlin. In 1933 he refused to collaborate with the Nazis and moved to the shores of Lake Constance. He was professor of photography and graphic art at the Hochschule für Bildende Künste in East Berlin from 1955 (**15, 19**).

Raoul Hausmann (1886-1971). Born in Vienna, he studied in Berlin where, in 1912, he joined the group Der Sturm. It was as a member of the Dada group that he made his first photomontages in 1918. In the 1920s, a period during which he became friendly with Moholy-Nagy, he was involved in various revolutionary and antimilitarist movements. In 1933 he left Nazi Germany and moved to Limoges in 1944, where he died, almost forgotten, in 1971 (**1, 3, 4**).

John Heartfield (1891-1968). Pseudonym (1916) of Helmut Herzfelde, born in Berlin. He met George Grosz, with whom he 'invented' photomontage and became a militant in the Berlin circles of the revolutionary avant-garde. A founder member of Dada in Berlin, he made book covers and designs for the Malik-Verlag and worked on political satirical journals (*Arbeiter Illustrierte Zeitung*); he stayed and exhibited in Moscow (1931-32). Obliged to leave Nazi Germany, he moved first to Prague and then to London, where he continued his artistic activities. From 1951 he was graphic designer for the Bertolt Brecht Theatre in Berlin (**9-14**).

Hannah Höch (1889-1978). She studied at the Berlin Kunstgewerbeschule and made her first abstract collages in 1916. Two years later she made photomontages alongside Raoul Hausmann. After meeting Hans Arp and Kurt Schwitters at the Der Sturm gallery she became involved in various Dadaist activities and, in 1920, she showed at the first international Dada exhibition in Berlin. In 1924 she met Mondrian in Paris, and then associated with the members of De Stijl in Holland between 1926 and 1929. She showed her photomontages at the exhibition 'Film und Foto' in Stuttgart in 1929 (**2, 6**).

Lajos Kassák (1887-1967). Hungarian. Poet, writer, very politically active, he was the founder of the magazine *MA* (*Today*). Having taken up painting in 1921, he made collages and photomontages in a Constructivist tradition (**41**).

Gustav Klucis (1895-1944). Born in Latvia. He trained in the studios of Malevich and Pevsner between 1918 and 1920, and taught at the Vkhutemas (technical studios for higher education in the fine arts) in 1920-21. During this period he made his first photomontages, posters and architectural drawings. A member of the Inkhuk (the Moscow institute for artistic culture), he made a large number of photomontages, applying the technique to postcards ('Spartakiades', 1928). The same year, he was one of the organizers of the October group, playing an active part in the photographic section until 1931. In 1938 he was interned in a camp where he died (**32, 33**).

Lajos Lengyel (1904-78). Hungarian. From 1919 he worked as a printer. He arrived in Budapest in 1927 and discovered the work of Moholy-Nagy. In 1930 he took his first photographs and then worked in advertising and on book covers. A great artist in the field of Hungarian printing, he was made director of the Kossuth printing works in Budapest in 1948 (**34-36**).

Alice Lex-Nerlinger (1893-1975). German. Studied at the Gewerbemuseum, Berlin. In 1919 she married the painter Oskar Nerlinger. She joined the German Communist Party (KPD) and the German Association of Revolutionary Visual Artists in 1928. This political involvement marked her work, which includes photomontages and photograms. From 1933 she lived in Italy, and returned to East Berlin after the war (**17**).

El Lissitzky (1890-1941). Russian. Studied architecture in Darmstadt (1909-1914), travelled to France and Italy and returned to Russia in 1914. He was very active as a graphic designer during the first years of the Revolution. His meetings with Chagall and particularly with Malevich led him towards Constructivist painting. He became one of its chief representatives with his series *Proun*. He began teaching at the Moscow Vkhutemas in 1921 and became a member of the October group in 1928. He was very closely associated with the avant-garde movements of Western Europe (Dada, De Stijl, Bauhaus), and organized representative exhibitions of Soviet revolutionary art ('Film und Foto', 1929, Stuttgart). He made great use of photomontage in the 1930s, but gradually turned away from artistic work (**29**).

Heinz Loew (b. 1903). German. He took the basic course at the Bauhaus, then worked on theatrical projects directed by Oskar Schlemmer in 1926 and 1927. With Joost Schmidt, he set up the studio for the visual arts (1927). He opened 'Studio Z' in Berlin in 1930. He emigrated to London in 1936 and then worked as an independent photographer (**16**).

Man Ray (1890-1977). American, real name Emmanuel Rudnitsky. A New York painter, he was a regular visitor to Stieglitz's 291 Gallery, where he encountered the work of the European avant-garde. Very impressed by the Armory Show, he became friendly with Duchamp, who was then in the USA. He published the only issue of *New York Dada* in 1921 and came to Paris, where he was involved with Dada activities. In 1922 he invented photograms or 'rayographs', and became a fashion photographer for the designer Paul Poiret. During the war he returned to the USA and went back to France in 1951 (**59**).

Làszlò Moholy-Nagy (1895-1946). Hungarian painter, sculptor, photographer, designer and theorist. He moved to Berlin in 1919, where he associated with the group Der Sturm and was influenced by Constructivism and El Lissitzky. In 1922, in collaboration with his wife Lucia Schultz, he made his first photograms; between 1923 and 1928 he taught at the Bauhaus (metalwork) and worked with Gropius on the series of 'Bauhausbücher'. He then worked as a designer and stage designer. Escaping from Nazism, he founded the New Bauhaus (1937), then the Institute of Design, in Chicago (**42-47**).

Vinicio Paladini (1902-71). Italian, self-taught painter. He discovered the avant-garde in 1921 by visiting Balla's studio. Close to the communist left and to Constructivism, he soon came to oppose Marinetti's fascist ideas and broke with the Futurists. In 1926 he set up the Imaginist movement. He made photomontages and book covers. He emigrated to the USA in 1935 (**49**).

Roger Parry (1905-77). French. He studied at the École des Beaux-Arts. In 1928 he met Maurice Tabard and started to work with *Arts et Métiers Graphiques*. His main experimental work is the illustrations to *Banalités* by Léon-Paul Fargue (1930), co-signed by Fabien Loris (**53**).

Kasimierz Podsadecki (1904-70). Polish. In 1923 he started making compositions of objects captured photographically (*Fotoformia*). A typographer, he made Constructivist photomontages published in magazines from 1928 onwards. From 1932 until 1934 he was involved in the Polish avant-garde cinema. After the war he painted post-Cubist compositions (**38**).

Alexander Rodchenko (1891-1956). Russian, born in St Petersburg. He met the Futurist poets Mayakovsky, Burliuk and Kamenski in 1914. He arrived in Moscow in 1915 and became interested in Malevich's Suprematism in 1916. Active during the Revolution, he was a member of the visual arts section of the People's Commissariat of Education. A teacher at the Vkhutemas, a painter and graphic designer, he made photomontages from 1923, then became a photographer (member of the October group) and a photo-journalist. At the beginning of the 1930s he was obliged to give up his activities, but devoted himself to producing books (**28, 30, 31**).

Kurt Schwitters (1887-1948). German. In Hanover he started out as a painter influenced by the avant-garde movements of the day (Futurism, Fauvism, Cubism, Blaue Reiter). In 1918 he made his first abstract paintings and made collages of elements found in the street. His montages finally invaded his flat, which he saw as a huge collage-building (*Merz-bau*). From 1920 he was involved in the Dada movement and set up his own magazine, *Merz*, in 1923. Close to the Bauhaus and De Stijl, he was a member of Abstraction-Creation. The photograph was one of his compositional elements. In 1937 he escaped to Norway and then to England (**5**).

Anton Stankowski (b. 1906). German. Studied photography and design between 1927 and 1929 with Max Burchartz at the Folkwangschule in Essen. He then made photograms. Until 1936 he was a graphic designer with an advertising company in Zurich. In 1937 he moved to Stuttgart as a photographer (**24**).

André Steiner (1901-78). Of Hungarian origin, he studied in Vienna and moved to Paris in 1927. An engineer, he worked as a professional photographer, publishing (albums of nudes in particular) in *Arts et Métiers Graphiques*, using experimental techniques (photograms, photomontages, superimposition) (**18**).

Maurice Tabard (1897-1984). French, he left for the USA in 1914 and studied photography at the New York Institute of Photography. A portraitist, he also worked on Surrealist compositions. Having returned to Paris in 1928, he met Philippe Soupault and Lucien Vogel (*VU* magazine). A fashion and advertising photographer, he worked on numerous magazines. In 1929 he featured in the exhibition 'Film und Foto' in Stuttgart. In 1946, at the request of Alexei Brodovitch, he worked for *Harper's Bazaar* in the USA. He died in Nice, the city to which he had retired (**56, 57**).

Umbo (1902-80). German, real name Otto Umbehr. After working in various jobs (designer, cameraman, writer, clown), he joined the Bauhaus in 1921. In 1923 he

stayed in Berlin and made posters and photomontages. In 1926 he became friends with Paul Citroen and started to work as a press photographer. At the end of his life he taught photography in Hildesheim and Hanover (**8**).

Dziga Vertov (1896-1954). Of Polish origin, real name Denis Arkadovič. After studying music and medicine in Moscow, in 1919 he made a film on the principle of montage, *The Anniversary of the Revolution*, and was a member of the film committee set up by the People's Commissariat. In 1929 he made *The Man with the Movie-Camera*. He was closely associated with Rodchenko, who designed the poster for his *Kino-Glas* in 1924 (**20**).

Moï Wer (b. 1904). Russian, real name Moses Worobeitschik. He studied at the Dessau Bauhaus in 1927, and then went to Paris in 1928. Often included in *Arts et Métiers Graphiques*, he published two books illustrated with photomontages: *Paris*, with a preface by Fernand Léger, and *Le Ghetto de Wilna* (1931) (**22, 23**).

Wanda Wulz (b. 1903). Italian, she first learned photography in her father's studio in Trieste, where she devoted herself to studio portraits from 1928. She joined the Futurists in 1931, and took part in the Trieste exhibition of Futurist photography in 1932. Her photomontages are in the line of Dada and Surrealism (**48**).

Piet Zwart (1885-1977). Dutch. Zwart was a graphic artist and designer associated with Mondrian and Van Doesburg's group De Stijl. In 1923, after meeting El Lissitzky, he made his first photograms. He taught in Rotterdam between 1919 and 1933, and at the Berlin Bauhaus in 1931. He used photography, photograms and photomontages for his advertising work, posters and books (**26, 27**).

GENERAL BIBLIOGRAPHY

Ades, Dawn, **Photomontage**, London and New York, Thames and Hudson, 1986.

Bauhaus Fotografie, Edition Marzona, 1982.

Bertonati, Emilio, **Das experimentelle Photo in Deutschland 1918-1940**, exhibition catalogue, Munich, Galleria del Levante, 1978.

Bouqueret, Christian, **Bauhaus photographie**, exhibition catalogue, Arles, Musée Réattu, and Paris, Musée d'Art moderne de la Ville, 1983.

Dada-Constructivism, the Janus Face of the Twenties, exhibition catalogue, London, Annely Juda Fine Art, 1984.

Dada Photomontagen, exhibition catalogue, Hanover, Kestner-Gesellschaft, 1979.

Evans, David and Sylvia Gohl, **Photomontage: A Political Weapon**, London, Gordon Fraser, 1986.

Film und Foto der zwanziger Jahre, exhibition catalogue, Stuttgart, Württembergischer Kunstverein, 1979.

Fotomontage, exhibition catalogue, Berlin, Kunstgewerbemuseum, 1931.

Giroud, Michel, texts and documents selected and introduced by, **Raoul Hausmann 'Je ne suis pas un photographe'**, Paris, Chêne, 1975.

Jaguer, Édouard, **Les Mystères de la Chambre noire**, Paris, Flammarion, 1982.

John Heartfield, photomontages antinazis, Paris, Chêne, 1978.

Jürgens-Kirchhoff, Annegret, **Technik und Tendenz der Montage in der bildenden Kunst des 20. Jahrhunderts**, Giessen (RFA), Anabas-Verlag Günter Kämpf KG, 1978.

Krauss, Rosalind, Jane Livingston and Dawn Ades, **Explosante fixe**, Paris, Centre Georges-Pompidou and Hazan, 1986.

Leclanche-Boulé, Claude, **Typographies et Photomontages constructivistes en U.R.S.S.**, Paris, Éditions Papyrus, 1984.

Lista, Giovanni, **Photographie futuriste italienne 1911-1939**, exhibition catalogue, Paris, Musée d'Art moderne de la Ville, 1982.

Paris Berlin, exhibition catalogue, Paris, Centre Georges-Pompidou, 1978.

Paris Moscou, exhibition catalogue, Paris, Centre Georges-Pompidou, 1978.

Présences polonaises, exhibition catalogue, Paris, Centre Georges-Pompidou, 1983.

Van Deren Coke, **1919-1939 Avant-Garde photographique en Allemagne**, Paris, Philippe Sers, 1982.

Wescher, Herta, **Die Geschichte der Collage**, Cologne, DuMont Verlag, 1974.

PHOTO CREDITS

PHOTOFILE

The Photofile series is conceived and produced
by the Centre National de la Photographie, Paris,
under the direction of Robert Delpire.